GERM HUNTER

A Creative Minds Biography

GERM HUNTER

A Story about Louis Pasteur

by Elaine Marie Alphin

illustrations by Elaine Verstraete

 Carolrhoda Books, Inc./Minneapolis

For Art, who, like Louis, spends long hours in his laboratory searching for answers to free the innocent   —E. M. A.

For MaryAnne, Mariah, Dave, Leif, Scott, Eric, Russ, Joe, and Jed   —E. V.

Carolrhoda Books, Inc.
A division of Lerner Publishing Group
241 First Avenue North
Minneapolis, MN 55401 U.S.A.

Website address: www.lernerbooks.com

Library of Congress Cataloging-in-Publication Data

Alphin, Elaine Marie.
     Germ hunter : a story about Louis Pasteur / by Elaine Marie Alphin ; illustrations by Elaine Verstraete.
          p.   cm. — (A creative minds biography)
     ISBN: 1–57505–179–6 (lib. bdg. : alk. paper)
     1. Pasteur, Louis, 1822–1895—Juvenile literature. 2. Scientists—France—Biography—Juvenile literature. 3. Microbiologists—France—Biography—Juvenile literature. [1. Pasteur, Louis, 1822–1895. 2. Microbiologists. 3. Scientists.] I. Verstraete, Elaine, ill. II. Title. III. Series.
     Q143.P2 A63 2003
     579'.092—dc21   2002004702

Manufactured in the United States of America
1 2 3 4 5 6 – JR – 08 07 06 05 04 03

Table of Contents

1

Someone Must Know
the Answer

Louis Pasteur heard shouts and looked up. He and his best friend, Jules Vercel, had been playing marbles near Louis's house in Arbois, France. The boys saw some villagers helping an injured man stagger to the blacksmith shop. The man's bare chest bled from ragged bites. Louis guessed what had happened. The mad wolf had struck again.

Eight-year-old Louis ran to the blacksmith shop with Jules. He watched the blacksmith pump the bellows to make his fire hotter. Within minutes an iron bar glowed red-hot in the coals. The blacksmith pressed the bar against the bites in the victim's chest. Horrified by the smell of burning flesh, Louis ran for home. The man's screams echoed in his ears.

That autumn eight people had been bitten by the mad wolf that roamed the countryside around Arbois. The creature's bites caused a terrible disease called rabies. In 1831 people didn't understand rabies well.

They believed that burning a victim's bites with red-hot iron could stop rabies before it killed. But most victims died from the bites anyway. They foamed at the mouth in agony, unable to swallow water. How did rabies kill? How could it be stopped?

Along with other eight-year-olds in Arbois, Louis had just entered first grade. He wished that his schoolmaster and his books could answer questions like these. His father, Jean-Joseph Pasteur, had promised Louis that he would learn great things in school. He hoped that Louis would go on to become a teacher and bring honor to the family.

Louis's father had little education. His own father had been a tanner, someone who treated animal skins with the tannin in oak bark to make them into leather. As a young man, Jean-Joseph planned to become a tanner, too. Then he was drafted into the army of Emperor Napoleon Bonaparte. Jean-Joseph served so well that he was awarded the cross of the Legion of Honor by the emperor himself—a great honor.

Every Sunday as Louis was growing up, Jean-Joseph would pin his Legion of Honor ribbon onto his old army coat. Then he took his son for long walks through the hilly vineyards surrounding Arbois. He told Louis about the history of France and about the honor and duty of serving one's country.

Louis promised he would carry on the family's honor by getting an education. He would make something of himself so he could serve his country and care for his family: his hardworking parents; his older sister, Virginie; and his younger sisters, Josephine and Emilie.

Despite his promises to his father, Louis couldn't seem to do well at school. While his teacher, Monsieur Renaud, droned on about spelling and math, Louis had trouble paying attention. Questions from the world outside his classroom puzzled him. How could you cure the bites of rabid wolves? How did oak bark turn animal skins into leather?

Louis wanted to find the answers to these questions—and to questions closer to home as well. Why was his little sister Josephine so weak? Why did she cough all the time? The doctors of the 1830s didn't know that Josephine had a disease called tuberculosis. They didn't know how to make the little girl well.

Louis also wondered about Emilie. Why did his smallest sister shudder violently and faint without warning? Emilie suffered from epilepsy, and doctors understood this disease even less than tuberculosis. Why did the doctors know so little?

Louis yearned to fill his school notebooks with his questions and their answers, but Monsieur Renaud had no answers to give him. Louis wished he could become a monitor. These boys took charge of their classmates and even gave them lessons. Did monitors have some special knowledge? If he became one, would he learn the things he wanted to know? But Monsieur Renaud never picked Louis to be a monitor. He thought the boy was dreamy—more like an artist than a scholar.

Louis did seem dreamy sometimes. Although he liked fishing with Jules, Louis often walked alone through the vineyards. He carried his pastel crayons and a pad of paper so he could sketch the scenes and people he saw. His drawings impressed some of his teachers, who wondered if he should become an artist.

Jean-Joseph was pleased his son could draw well. But he also encouraged Louis to do better in Arbois College, the middle school Louis now attended. His earlier teachers had written him off as a slow student. But the Arbois headmaster, Monsieur Romanet, thought differently. Seeing Louis walking by himself while the other boys played, Monsieur Romanet sometimes joined him.

As they talked, the teacher made a discovery. Louis wasn't slow, by any means. His mind carefully explored the questions that troubled him. And when he was asked a new question, Louis would examine it carefully from every angle before giving his answer.

His imagination sometimes came up with ideas that Monsieur Romanet never heard from his other students. Louis weighed these unusual ideas against more common answers before choosing one. Once he made his choice, he stuck to it stubbornly and argued for it with passion.

During their walks, Monsieur Romanet explained his thoughts about learning. He believed that true education was not memorizing schoolbooks, as the Arbois teachers required. True education meant learning how the facts in the schoolbooks came to be known. To get this sort of training, a student would have to go to a university. With such an education, a scholar could discover solutions to problems and share them with others.

Louis was delighted. This was exactly what he had hoped school would teach him—how to discover answers to his own questions.

But a student had to earn good grades to get into a university. Thirteen-year-old Louis threw himself into the schoolwork his teachers wanted him to master. In both seventh and eighth grade, the student that teachers had thought was slow walked away with all the academic prizes. Monsieur Romanet told Jean-Joseph that Louis should try for admittance to the Ecole Normale Supérieure in Paris. This university had been founded by Emperor Napoleon to train promising students to become teachers.

Jean-Joseph wasn't sure this was the best plan. Louis had never been away from home. Besides, the Ecole Normale Supérieure was expensive. Perhaps Louis should attend school in nearby Besançon. Then he would be qualified to become a teacher in Arbois. That achievement would be impressive enough.

Then a family friend from Paris suggested another plan. He could keep an eye on Louis if the boy came to the city. And instead of leaving home and family for one of the hardest universities in France, Louis could start at an easier school. Classes at the Barbet school in Paris would prepare him to go the Ecole Normale Supérieure later. The Barbet school cost less, also.

Jean-Joseph finally agreed. Louis was eager to begin to learn how to answer the questions that puzzled him. But he worried about traveling so far from home. At least he wouldn't have to go alone. Jules would also be studying in Paris. As long as he had his friend, Louis thought he would be all right.

Rain and sleet pelted Louis and Jules as the boys boarded the stagecoach to Paris in 1838. But fifteen-year-old Louis promised himself he would feel at home in the city as soon as he began to study.

2

Will, Work, and Success

Louis was wrong. He tried to study at the Barbet school, but he lay awake nights missing his home. He told Jules, "If I could smell the tannery yard, I feel I should be cured."

Aware of the boy's misery but unable to cheer him, Monsieur Barbet wrote to the Pasteurs. One November morning, Louis was called from his studies. He was told that someone wanted him. It was Jean-Joseph, who simply said, "I have come to bring you home."

Louis was overjoyed to return to Arbois, but he was also confused. Did his failure in Paris mean that he would never become a real scholar? Would he never bring honor to his family as a teacher? He spent long hours sketching townspeople and friends, and he returned to Arbois College to continue studying.

In the spring of 1839, Louis again took all the school prizes. One year after his failure in Paris, he felt ready to leave home again. But Paris was too far away. Perhaps the route to the Ecole Normale Supérieure lay through the school at Besançon, after all.

Louis plunged into his studies at Besançon enthusiastically. At age seventeen, he passed an important series of tests. His teachers thought he was "good" in subjects such as Greek, Latin, history, philosophy, and writing. But they noted that he was "very good" in science.

Louis was no longer homesick. Instead, he was fascinated by his studies. Mastering science, he realized, would make him able to answer the questions that troubled him. If he worked hard enough, surely he would succeed. He wrote home advising his sisters, "These three things, Will, Work, [and] Success, fill human existence. Will opens the door to a brilliant and happy career; Work takes you through the door; and at the end of the journey Success crowns your efforts."

Louis could send home money as well as letters because he was now earning an income. He had finally become a monitor. But despite his hard work and optimism, he failed his next series of tests.

He stopped writing letters with advice. Instead, Louis wrote home, "You have your troubles, but so do

I, and mine grow bigger every day." He spent extra time on his hardest subjects, even those he disliked. Finally he passed his tests in 1842.

The next step would be to take still more tests, this time for acceptance to the Ecole Normale Supérieure. Louis studied for twelve hours a day. Science became his passion. He wrote home that his chemistry teacher, Jean-Baptiste Dumas, "could set fire to the soul."

Louis's hard work paid off. In 1843 he was admitted to the Ecole Normale Supérieure. At last he had entered the world of scientific investigation!

He began working as a laboratory assistant to chemist Jérôme Balard. His first important project concerned two sets of crystals. They appeared to be identical. But one set of crystals reflected light in a certain way. The other set reflected light differently. No one could figure out why.

Louis was working on this puzzle when his mother suffered a stroke in Arbois. He rushed home, only to find that she had already died. Heartbroken, he could not work for weeks.

Burying himself in his research again, Louis made an extraordinary discovery. His two crystals were not really identical. Looking carefully through a microscope, Louis saw that one crystal was actually a mirror image of the other. The two crystals reflected light differently because they *were* different!

This discovery excited Louis. A person could apply the same force, like light, to two things that looked the same. But if those things were different inside—even if the difference was hard to see at first—the force would act on them differently. Could Louis apply this discovery to forces other than light, such as heat or cold? And could he apply it to things other than crystals—like whatever unknown things caused diseases? No scientist had seen this possibility before.

Louis showed his discovery to Jean-Baptiste Biot, a famous scientist. Biot took Louis by the arm and said, "I love science so deeply that this stirs my heart." Soon Biot became Louis's mentor, guiding and supporting him in his work.

Despite his success at the Ecole Normale Supérieure, Louis had trouble finding a teaching job in Paris after his graduation in 1848. He had disliked Paris when he was fifteen, but at twenty-six he realized that the city was the center of scientific research. Unfortunately, the closest job he could find was in Dijon, more than a hundred miles away.

Louis was now a teacher, as his father had hoped he would become. But his students kept him too busy to do his own experiments. In January 1849, he got a better job at a university in Strasbourg. Strasbourg was still far from Paris, but Louis came to like it much better. It was there that he fell in love with a warm, gentle woman named Marie Laurent.

In February Louis begged his father to write to Marie's father. This was the way families arranged marriages. But Louis was too impatient to wait. Determined to win Marie, he wrote to Monsieur Laurent himself, asking for her hand. Then he wrote to Marie, promising her, "Time will show you that below my cold, shy and unpleasing exterior, there is a heart full of affection for you!"

Monsieur Laurent let his daughter decide. Marie asked herself whether she could marry this intense young man who was much more at home in the laboratory than the parlor. In the end, she decided she could.

For five years, Louis and Marie lived in Strasbourg. Louis worked long hours in the classroom and in his laboratory, continuing his research on crystals. In the evenings, he discussed his work with Marie. Listening to him with all her heart, Marie learned so much about crystals and chemistry that she was able to write up his notes about his experiments.

Louis became a father as well as a husband. He and Marie had a son and two daughters, and shared the work of raising them. Unlike many fathers of the time, Louis even got up at night when the babies cried.

Then, in 1854, Louis was named dean, or head, of the new science department at the University of Lille. At thirty-two, he was the youngest dean at any university in France. The university didn't want its scientists spending all their time investigating ideas and theories in the laboratory. Instead, they should also do practical work that would solve problems for farmers and business owners. And like scientists at other universities, they should teach their students to put their theories to the test as well. This blending of theory and practical work was exactly what Louis wanted for his career.

Louis's students took home enthusiastic tales of his lectures and experiments. Monsieur Bigo, whose son was in Louis's class, wondered if the new dean could solve his problem. He produced alcohol at his factory by adding yeast to sugar beets in large tanks called vats. But this process, known as fermentation, was going wrong somehow. The liquid in many vats was turning sour instead of fermenting properly. Perhaps the dean could help? Louis agreed to try.

The beets and yeast seemed the same in both the healthy vats and the sour vats. But Louis remembered that scientists had thought his two sets of crystals seemed the same also. Was there a difference here that no one else had seen? He paced, ignoring everyone around him, thinking only about the scientific problem. He spent such long hours in his laboratory that Marie wrote to her father, "He is now up to his neck in beet juice."

Part of Louis's challenge was that scientists didn't know exactly what yeasts were. A few people had observed that yeasts seemed to be alive, but no one was sure what role they played in fermentation. Looking at samples from the healthy vats through his microscope, Louis confirmed that they contained living yeasts. He realized that yeasts were microbes, living things that are so tiny they can be seen only with a microscope.

But what was wrong with the sour-smelling vats? Louis studied samples from those vats under his microscope as well. He didn't see any yeasts at all. Instead, he saw long rods—and they were multiplying quickly. Could the rods be alive also?

Louis took a new approach to research. Other scientists started from what they knew to be true and tried to reason out what they didn't understand. Louis started from an imaginative guess, then tested it to see if it was correct. He guessed that the rods were harmful microbes, called germs, that prevented fermentation. And he guessed that yeasts were helpful microbes that caused fermentation.

Sure enough, he didn't find any rods in the healthy vats. He told Monsieur Bigo to destroy the vats with rods and to use only the healthy vats. The advice worked. Once all the rods were eliminated, Monsieur Bigo's alcohol no longer soured. Louis knew that he didn't understand fermentation completely yet, but he had made an important start. What would other scientists think of his ideas?

3

Arguments and Proof

Jean-Baptiste Biot, Louis's mentor from the Ecole Normale Supérieure, thought Louis's ideas were an important new discovery. He tried to get Louis elected to the Academy of Science, a great honor that would advance his career. New members of the academy were elected by existing members. If Louis got elected, it would mean that other scientists agreed about the importance of his research. But Louis got only sixteen of the thirty votes he needed for election.

Discouraged, he went back to work. Now he searched for microbes in sour milk and spoiled butter. Again he saw microbes—different ones than the rods responsible for the sour beets. Louis concluded that healthy milk or butter went bad, like beet juice, when a unique, harmful type of microbe—a germ—got into them. That germ produced more and more germs like itself until they made the milk or butter spoil.

In order to share his ideas effectively, Louis realized he must move to Paris. That was where the nation's most important scientists lived. He got a new job as director of scientific studies at the Ecole Normale Supérieure. In 1857 the growing Pasteur family (a new baby was on the way) moved to Paris. Now surrounded by other scientists, Louis hoped that discussion of microbes would lead to further research on germs and how to control them.

Unfortunately, Louis's new job didn't come with a laboratory for his experiments. He spent more than two thousand francs of his own money to transform a school attic into a makeshift laboratory. It was cold in winter, but Louis wrote his old friend Jules Vercel, "I have grown accustomed to my attic, and I should be sorry to leave it. . . . Let these hindrances [challenges] stimulate us, rather than discourage us."

The cold attic laboratory wasn't the only challenge Louis faced. Instead of agreeing with him about the way germs spoiled food, many scientists, called naturalists, had other ideas. Their disagreement stimulated Louis to pursue the question of where microbes came from and to prove he was right.

Naturalists believed in a theory known as spontaneous generation. This was the idea that organisms, or living things, could come from nonliving things.

For example, naturalists thought that maggots were created by rotting meat. After all, they never saw maggots anywhere except on rotting meat. The Italian scientist Francesco Redi had shown back in 1668 that flies were attracted to rotting meat. They laid eggs on the meat, and the eggs hatched into maggots. But most people didn't believe Redi's research.

Naturalists believed that spontaneous generation explained the germs that Louis had found in sour beets and milk. According to the naturalists, beets and milk created germs as they soured. Louis disagreed. He thought that microbes, including germs, lived in the air. They settled into beets or milk or meat because that material fed the microbes. The food then allowed them to reproduce.

In 1859 a naturalist named Félix-Archimède Pouchet challenged Louis to prove his argument. Louis began a detailed series of experiments. He was careful to set them up precisely and wouldn't let anyone else touch his equipment. In fact, he was so possessive of his work that some scientists found him irritating. But Louis's care made the results of his experiments more reliable than theirs.

First Louis mixed a liquid called a nutrient solution, which he hoped would feed many different types of microbes. It was indeed soon full of tiny organisms.

He mixed the same solution again, then sterilized it by boiling it. Sterilization killed all the microbes the solution contained.

Next Louis melted the mouth of the flask closed to keep air out. If air contained microbes, as Louis believed, the microbes would not be able to enter the flask. Sure enough, no microbes grew. Louis unsealed the mouth of the flask and left it open to the air. Microbes soon flourished.

While Louis worked, Marie and their daughters visited Arbois. Then, in August, Marie wrote that Louis must come quickly—nine-year-old Jeanne had caught typhoid fever. By the time he arrived, Jeanne had died. Heartbroken, Louis became even more determined to understand germs. He guessed they did more than sour milk and butter. Louis suspected that germs also fed on tissues inside the human body and were the cause of diseases and death. He must discover where germs came from and how to stop them. And he must make the naturalists listen to him, starting with Pouchet.

Despite Louis's experiments, Pouchet still insisted that air didn't carry germs. He believed that air kept them alive. After all, germs were living things, and all living things need air. As Pouchet saw it, the nutrient solution in Louis's sealed flask could have created germs that died from lack of air. The absence of germs didn't mean that none had been created by the solution. It just meant that the germs had died.

To disprove this idea, Louis devised another experiment. He poured his nutrient solution into a long-necked flask, then melted the neck into a curve. After sterilizing the solution, he left it open to the air. Air could now enter the flask and reach the solution in the bottom. If the solution created germs, there would be plenty of air to feed them.

But Louis believed that no germs would grow in the solution because of the shape of the flask's neck. Germs were carried by air currents, but they had no way to move through still air on their own. Louis expected that any germs carried by the air into the flask would not be able to move through the curved neck to the nutrient solution. They would simply drop to the bottom of the flask's neck.

As Louis predicted, no germs grew in the flask with the curved neck. Pouchet had been wrong. A nutrient solution couldn't create germs.

Carrying his work further in 1860, Louis sealed his nutrient solution in many flasks. He broke open their necks under different conditions, then resealed them after they had been exposed to the microbes in the air. He opened some of the flasks in crowded city streets.

All those flasks filled with microbes. But only a few flasks caught microbes from the air in a closed cellar, or from the air high in the Alps. Here was another proof that microbes lived in the air. Many microbes crowded the city air, where there was more food for them to grow and reproduce. Fewer microbes lived where there was little to feed them.

Louis dared Pouchet to disprove his experiments. Pouchet tried but could not. In December 1862, Louis finally won election to the Academy of Science. At last, at the age of forty, he had been recognized by the scientists he most admired.

Jean-Baptiste Dumas, the chemist who had set fire to Louis's soul years before at the Barbet school, presented the new member of the academy to Emperor Napoleon III in 1863. Louis told his emperor, "My whole ambition is to arrive at an understanding of the causes of . . . diseases." Pleased, the emperor encouraged him.

Napoleon's support meant that he might give Louis money to build a larger laboratory. But it also meant that Louis had to respond to the emperor's requests. When Napoleon commanded him to interrupt his research to solve a national problem, he had no choice but to agree.

4

Unwelcome Requests

Emperor Napoleon III had heard too many complaints about French wine. France was famous for its vineyards, and the sale of wine was one of the nation's most important businesses. But lately French wines had tasted sour or bitter. While winemakers claimed that crushing and blending the grapes was an art, Napoleon suspected it was a science. He hoped that the scientist who had cracked the mystery of fermentation could solve the mystery of French wines going bad.

Louis was still busy with his germ research, but he reminded himself that being a scientist often meant investigating multiple questions at once. In 1864 he left Marie and their four children in Paris. (The newest baby, Camille, was only one year old.) Louis returned to Arbois, hoping to learn more about wine from the vineyards he had explored as a child. He set up a laboratory and hired an assistant.

In winemaking Louis recognized a familiar process. As wine aged in vats, it fermented, like beets. Louis wondered if a unique germ could be responsible for changing the taste of the wine—like the rod-shaped germs that soured the beets he had studied.

Looking at good wines and sour wines under his microscope, Louis saw different microbes in each. All the wines contained healthy microbes that helped their flavor improve as they aged. But the sour wines also contained unhealthy microbes—germs—that changed their taste. Louis already knew that heating a liquid enough would kill any microbes it contained. But how could he kill the germs without destroying the healthy microbes?

Louis remembered what he had discovered about the two sets of crystals. A force like light or heat would act differently on different things. He experimented until he found the force he needed—heat. He told winemakers to heat the wine at 135°F for a few minutes before bottling it. That temperature was hot enough to kill the germs without harming the healthy microbes. This heating process was called pasteurization, after Louis. It would be used, in time, to kill germs in milk as well as in wine.

When the emperor first asked Louis to save France's wine business, Louis had been irritated because the work would take him away from his research on the germs that caused diseases in people. But now he saw a connection. Applying the force of heat to wine had stopped germs from ruining it. Could Louis apply a similar force to the germs that attacked the human body? Could such a force stop diseases from killing people?

Napoleon III knew how much Louis wanted to understand the cause of diseases in people. The emperor hoped that Louis would be willing to study a disease that attacked a different creature. France's economy depended on the silk industry as well as the wine industry, and silkworms were dying at a fearful rate from a disease called pébrine. The emperor had Jean-Baptiste Dumas ask Louis to cure the silkworms as he had cured the wines. Louis sent an impatient reply that the request "troubles and embarrasses me! Remember, if you please, that I have never even touched a silkworm."

But when Dumas—and the emperor—gently insisted, Louis set off for Alès to meet the silkworm breeders and touch his first silkworm caterpillar. These caterpillars create silk by spinning cocoons. They hatch from eggs laid by silkworm moths. Seeing them, Louis felt uncertain. His background was in crystals and fermentation, not animal studies.

He could shatter a crystal to examine it or look at microbes under a microscope. But the thought of cutting open an animal to study it seemed horrible.

Still, he had a job to do. He overcame his squeamishness about using animals in experiments. In 1865 he examined sickly silkworms, looking for microbes in their body tissue. Young caterpillars didn't have any microbes that Louis could see. But microbes did develop as the unhealthy caterpillars grew.

Louis guessed that the microbes were passed from silkworm moth parents to their caterpillar young. To test his idea, he told the silkworm breeders to isolate each pair of moth parents just before the female laid her eggs. The breeders should cut open the adult moths after the eggs were laid. Then they should grind up part of the tissue and examine it under a microscope. If the adults had the dangerous microbes, then the eggs were diseased and should be destroyed. If there was no sign of them, then the eggs were healthy.

Before Louis learned the results of this experiment, he got word that his father was dying. He rushed to Arbois in June, arriving too late to say good-bye. Three months later, baby Camille died of a liver tumor. In a lifetime of research, Louis had learned nothing that could save those he loved.

He returned to Alès, only to learn that his silkworm test hadn't worked. Diseased caterpillars had hatched from apparently healthy eggs. He had failed to guess the true cause of the disease.

Louis recalled his father bringing him home from Paris when he was a boy. He had failed then, also. But he had not given up. He had studied harder and made it to the Ecole Normale Supérieure. He must not give up now.

Then, in May 1866, twelve-year-old Cécile died of typhoid fever. Grief-stricken, Louis wrote to Marie, "So they will all die, one by one, our dear children." Refusing to be parted from his family any longer, Louis found a house in Alès and brought Marie and their remaining daughter from Paris to join him, leaving their son at school.

Marie and eight-year-old Marie-Louise joined the routine of caring for the silkworms and examining the moths under the microscope. Seeing Marie-Louise use a microscope so confidently encouraged the breeders to master the tool themselves.

Louis paced in his laboratory, pondering the problem of pébrine. He realized that the microbes he had been studying weren't germs. They were parasites, tiny organisms that attacked healthy animals and lived on or inside their bodies. The parasites were not just passed on from parents to eggs. The disease was contagious, meaning that the parasites could spread from a diseased caterpillar to a healthy one.

But Louis still had not seen the whole picture. Two more years passed before he realized that a deadly combination of pébrine and a second, different, disease threatened France's silkworms.

The second disease was called flacherie. Louis examined caterpillars and the mulberry leaves they ate under his microscope. He finally realized that flacherie germs grew in the folds and creases of the leaves. If a healthy caterpillar ate those leaves, it would get sick. Like pébrine, flacherie was contagious. By keeping the caterpillars' food clean and separating infected caterpillars from healthy ones, breeders could stop the cycle of disease.

Louis and his family returned to Paris, where the emperor was having a new laboratory built for him to thank him for his service to France. Louis was about to present a report on silkworms to the Academy of Science in October 1868 when he felt unwell. That night he suffered a stroke and was paralyzed.

Louis's condition improved over the next few days. He remained alert and could speak at times, but he couldn't move. The emperor sent a servant every day to ask after him, and Marie and his friends stayed close. A week after the stroke, Louis managed to dictate a detailed note to the academy about silkworms. But he recalled his mother's stroke and told Marie that he feared he was dying. He asked her to tell the emperor that he was "filled with regret that I have not done enough to honor his reign."

By November, though, it was clear that Louis was not dying. He listened to his friends read to him, and he asked daily about progress on his laboratory. Learning that work had been stopped when he had his stroke, Louis sent a furious complaint to the emperor that he was being buried too soon. At age forty-seven, he still had plenty of work to do before he died. Work on the laboratory restarted immediately.

It took two months for Louis to learn to walk again. His left leg and arm remained slightly paralyzed. He would have to trust his assistants with delicate experiments that took two hands. This was hard for Louis. He had always liked to do all his experimental work himself. He had never even allowed his assistants to keep his records, only Marie. Now he would have to rely on others, too. At least Louis's brain—and his right hand—were still strong and healthy.

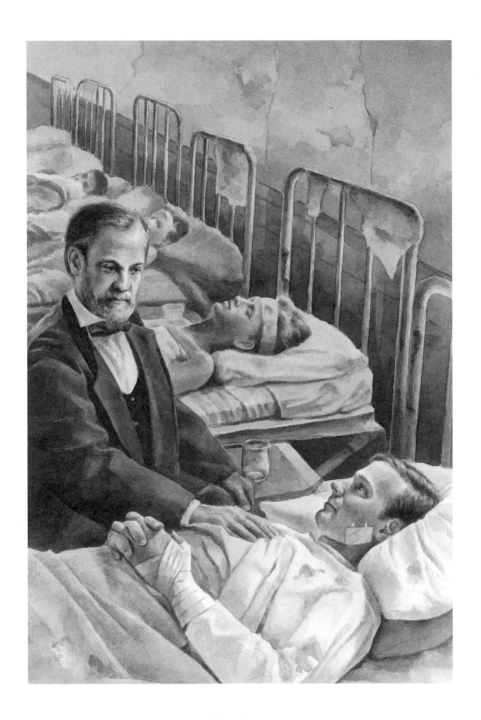

5

At War with Germs

The year 1870 brought changes for both France and Louis's work. Germany attacked France, claiming that two French provinces on the German border should become part of Germany. Because of his paralysis, Louis could not take part in the war that resulted. But his son, Jean-Baptiste, fought in the army. Many French soldiers were shot, but Jean-Baptiste was struck down by typhoid fever instead of a bullet. Typhoid was even more frightening than bullets to Louis. He had already lost two daughters to the disease.

Jean-Baptiste was recovering when his father visited him in the hospital. Louis was shocked by the rotten stench of germs growing in open wounds. Years of work had convinced him that germs caused diseases—and the hospital was so filthy that germs must be spreading rapidly. But the hospital's doctors wouldn't listen to him. He might be a scientist who had saved France's wine and cured the silkworms, but he had never studied medicine.

To convince doctors of the danger of germs, Louis knew he had to earn their respect. So he campaigned for election to the Academy of Medicine and was admitted in 1873. Immediately he proposed that doctors wash their hands and tools before operating on patients, not just afterward. He recommended sterile operating rooms. He urged doctors to put on clean smocks before seeing each patient, instead of working with one patient after another in the same blood-spattered smock.

Even though Louis was now a member of their academy, many French doctors refused to listen to him. But a doctor in Scotland had followed his research closely. Joseph Lister had seen how wounds became infected after air entered them. He was convinced that the germs Louis described must be the reason. Lister attempted to sterilize his patients' wounds as well as the hospital surroundings. The number of healthy survivors increased.

In 1874 Lister wrote to thank Louis for his "brilliant researches." That same year, the French government voted to give Louis a yearly income in honor of his help to the nation. He was grateful. He had had to give up his teaching position after his stroke, and the Pasteurs needed the money.

Slowly, some French doctors adopted more sterile methods in their hospitals. But other doctors still believed that spontaneous generation was responsible for the appearance of germs in wounds. Before Louis could convince these doctors that he was right, a different disease crossed his path.

Anthrax is a contagious disease that typically strikes livestock like sheep and cows, killing within hours after an animal becomes sick. Humans who come into contact with sick animals can catch the disease as well, though this is rare. By 1877 anthrax had become so widespread in French sheep that the government asked Louis to study the disease.

Louis attacked the case with his microscope and his imagination. Examining blood from sheep that had died of anthrax, he found a germ that he believed was responsible. How could he stop the disease? He knew that an English doctor, Edward Jenner, had successfully stopped the spread of a human disease called smallpox. Jenner had injected healthy people with pus from a sore caused by cowpox, a cow disease similar to smallpox. Those people were then safe from smallpox.

No one knew why the cowpox pus, called a vaccine, worked, but it did. Was there a way to protect animals from anthrax with a vaccine?

While Louis pondered this question, he gave his permission for his daughter, Marie-Louise, to marry. Jean-Baptiste had already married, so the Pasteur household dwindled back to Louis and Marie.

Louis remained absorbed in his research. In addition to helping him with his notes, Marie handled all the household finances. She even tucked the day's spending money into Louis's pockets when he went to the laboratory in the morning. Louis wrote to his son, "The wife makes the husband. Every couple that succeeds in life is served by a warmhearted and energetic woman."

Louis reported his ideas about anthrax to the Academy of Medicine. A veterinarian in the academy, Gabriel Colin, argued stubbornly against every point he made, even the simplest ones. When Louis observed that chickens didn't get anthrax, Colin claimed that they did. Louis then asked Colin to show him a chicken that had died of anthrax.

When Colin finally admitted he couldn't kill a

chicken with anthrax, Louis announced that he would try. The next week he presented the academy with a cage that contained two live chickens—and one dead one. He explained that the dead one had died from anthrax, but under very special circumstances.

That chicken died after a cold bath. Louis had realized that some unique condition must make it impossible for anthrax germs to grow in chickens. From his earlier studies with beets, he knew that all microbes need the right things to eat. From his work pasteurizing wine, he knew that they need the right temperature. The chicken had blood and internal organs, like a sheep or a rabbit, so the anthrax germs had enough to eat. Could a chicken's higher body temperature be the reason the germs could not survive in its body?

To find out, Louis had injected anthrax into one chicken, then plunged it into cold water to lower its temperature. It died. Then Louis injected one of the other two chickens without giving it a cold bath. It still stayed healthy. A third chicken got just a cold bath without an injection, to prove that cold water hadn't killed the first chicken. It lived. Body temperature *was* the key!

How could Louis use what he had learned about chickens and anthrax germs to help other livestock?

He couldn't raise the body temperature of sheep or cows to a chicken's temperature—that would harm the animals.

While Louis considered the problem, one of his assistants, Emile Roux, made an important discovery. Roux was studying another type of germ, chicken cholera. When he injected chickens with fresh cholera germs, the chickens died. Then he tried exposing the germs to oxygen. Chickens injected with these germs got a little sick but then got better. Next Roux injected fresh cholera germs into the same chickens. The birds didn't get sick at all. The oxygen-treated germs had protected them. Roux had discovered a way to create a cholera vaccine!

Louis realized that the oxygen had weakened the cholera germs. Could it weaken anthrax as well? He eagerly tried the experiment on rabbits, but it failed. He still hadn't found the right force.

Then Louis remembered the chicken that had died after a cold bath. Instead of killing anthrax germs by raising the body temperature of sheep and cows, maybe he could raise the temperature of the germs themselves. After all, heating wines to just the right temperature killed the germs that ruined them. Perhaps heating the anthrax germs could weaken them enough to create a vaccine.

After many experiments, Louis was sure he had succeeded. If he heated anthrax germs to a precise temperature for eight days, he could inject them into sheep, rabbits, or guinea pigs, and the animals wouldn't get sick.

Further experiments showed how to make the vaccine stronger and weaker. Louis got the best results if he first injected the animals with a weak solution, then injected them with a stronger solution. After that, he could inject them with full-strength anthrax and they would stay healthy.

Louis presented his findings to the Academy of Medicine in March 1881. Within days a veterinarian from Melun challenged Louis to a public test of his vaccine. Over the objections of his friends and his assistants that too many things could go wrong, Louis accepted the challenge. "What has succeeded in the laboratory on fourteen sheep," he promised, "will succeed just as well at Melun on fifty."

Louis had his assistants publicly inject twenty-five sheep and six cows with his vaccine in May 1881. They waited two weeks, then gave them the second, stronger dose. Two weeks later, they injected full-strength anthrax germs into the animals. They also injected the anthrax into a group of twenty-five sheep and four cows that had not received the vaccine.

After the last injection, one vaccinated lamb was feverish, and five other vaccinated sheep looked sick. Had Louis's assistants made a mistake with the doses? In his anxiety, Louis accused them of trying to ruin his work. Marie stepped in and quieted him down.

Louis hadn't needed to worry. On June 2, the test ended. The vaccinated animals were all still standing—the six ill sheep had recovered. Eighteen of the unvaccinated group were dead, and the rest were dying. As the growing crowd cheered, Louis triumphantly urged the doctors to wait three more days to be sure that none of the vaccinated animals died.

But he spoke too soon. One vaccinated ewe died on June 4. Louis ordered a public examination of the corpse. The examination proved that the ewe died from a pregnancy that went wrong, not from anthrax.

Farmers began using Louis's vaccine on their livestock with great success—but not complete success. A few of the tens of thousands of treated animals died because Louis's vaccine was not completely pure. Sometimes it contained microbes of other diseases that Louis hadn't yet identified. People were still grateful for the vaccine, but Louis would remember those deaths when he was ready to test his first human vaccine.

6

The Prepared Mind

While Louis worked on anthrax in 1880, waves of disease—the plague, cholera, and yellow fever—attacked people throughout Europe. Louis wondered about the microbes that caused these illnesses. Before he could research them, however, a doctor came to see him about a disease closer to home—rabies.

Louis remembered rabies from his childhood. Now a five-year-old boy lay suffering from this painful disease in the hospital. Louis could offer no suggestions, and the boy died the next day. Could Louis find the germ that was responsible?

He knew that rabies affected the way the brain worked. Perhaps the rabies germ attacked the brain directly. His assistants removed brain matter from dogs who had died of rabies, then injected healthy dogs with it. Louis felt sorry for the muzzled animals when they whimpered on the operating table. He insisted that they be drugged to make them sleep through the operation without feeling any pain.

In time the infected dogs showed symptoms of rabies. After they died, Louis examined their brain tissue under his microscope. He couldn't see any germs that seemed to be linked to rabies. But the dogs had clearly been infected with rabies from brain tissue. The germ must be too small to see. Still, Louis was sure it was there.

Louis wanted to create a weaker form of the disease to vaccinate dogs so that they wouldn't catch rabies. But what force could he apply to unseen germs to weaken them? Perhaps changing the quality of the germs' oxygen would work.

Louis hung a piece of tissue that he believed contained rabies germs in a flask. Beneath the tissue he put some caustic potash, a substance that causes drying. He then plugged the neck of the flask with sterile cotton. The air in the flask dried out.

A series of experiments showed that the rabies germs became weaker in very dry air. Louis injected these weaker germs into dogs and rabbits. They didn't get sick. Then he injected the test animals with full-strength rabies. They still stayed healthy. Louis had found a vaccine that prevented rabies!

Louis knew that he couldn't possibly vaccinate every dog and wolf for rabies. Perhaps it would be more practical to find a way to kill the disease after a person or animal had been infected.

Louis experimented with a series of injections, each one a little stronger than the one before. To his delight, he discovered a sequence of injections that prevented an animal that had already been infected with rabies from coming down with the disease. But would this cure work on a person? In March 1885, Louis wrote to his old friend Jules Vercel, "I have not yet dared to treat humans bitten by rabid dogs; but the time is not far off, and I would really like to begin with [testing the treatment on] myself . . . for I am beginning to feel very sure of my results."

Louis didn't have time to use himself as a test subject. That June a doctor asked him to help a ten-year-old girl suffering from rabies. Julie-Antoinette Poughon had been bitten on her upper lip by her dog. Rabies had rushed through her system. Louis had to make a terrible decision. Should he try his series of injections on the girl? What if she died, as a few sheep had died from impure doses of his anthrax vaccine?

Throughout his career, many people had asked Louis to help them. Often their requests seemed to take him in directions he had never intended to explore. Monsieur Bigo had asked him to look at vats of fermenting beets. The emperor had asked him to cure silkworms and solve the mystery of sour wine.

Each unexpected request had helped Louis understand microbes better. Each had led him directly down the path toward a confrontation with the germs that caused human disease.

Was it only by chance that his research had taken these steps? Louis once said, "Did you ever observe to whom accidents happen? Chance favors only the prepared mind." He had been successful so far because each request had prepared him to take the next step on his journey of investigation.

Louis decided he would try to save Julie-Antoinette's life. He told the doctor to give her the first injection. The next day, Louis rushed to the hospital to oversee the second injection, but the girl had died. He had failed.

Horrified at the girl's death, Louis examined her brain. He injected lab rabbits with tissue containing her rabies microbes. The rabbits died quickly, which showed that the rabies was advanced. Perhaps his injections were not a failure—perhaps he had been called in too late to have any chance of saving the girl.

Before these experiments were done, Louis got a second request. Nine-year-old Joseph Meister had been savagely bitten by a rabid dog on July 4. Instead of going to a doctor, his mother brought him to Louis two days later. She begged the scientist to help her son.

Louis still believed in his injections. Would they stand a better chance of success because Joseph's bites were recent? Without the injections, the boy would almost certainly die. Louis agreed to try to cure him.

Louis insisted that he could treat Joseph best if he could control his environment—hospitals still weren't sterile enough to be safe. So Joseph stayed with Louis and Marie. He got thirteen injections in ten days, each stronger than the one before.

The last injection contained the strongest form of rabies created in the laboratory. The night before it was given to Joseph, Marie wrote to Marie-Louise and Jean-Baptiste, "Your father has had another bad night; he is dreading the last inoculations [injections] on the child. And yet there can be no drawing back now!"

The night after Joseph received the last injection, Louis paced, unable to sleep. He had done everything he could to defeat rabies and save the boy, but the last injection was so strong that it would kill a laboratory animal in only seven days. Would Joseph live or die?

In a week, Louis had the answer. Joseph Meister lived. After this success, Louis was convinced that his rabies treatment worked. He was asked to help Jean-Baptiste Jupille, a fifteen-year-old shepherd from Arbois who had been bitten by a rabid dog.

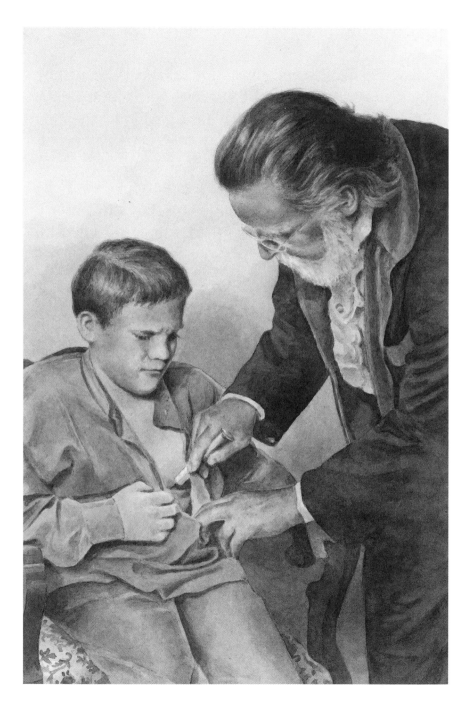

Louis didn't hesitate. After Jean-Baptiste recovered, anyone bitten by a rabid dog rushed to Louis.

Not every treatment was a success. Louis failed to save ten-year-old Louise Pelletier. Her parents waited over a month to bring her to him, and although he agreed to give her the full course of injections, she died. The doctors who had challenged Louis about anthrax used this failure to argue that his rabies treatment was no good. But the Pelletiers blamed themselves for not bringing Louise sooner. Her father praised Louis. He had risked his career and reputation to try to save their child, even knowing the odds were against him.

Despite his critics, rabies victims flocked to Louis from all over the world for his treatment. By the end of 1886, it had saved more than 2,500 people. After a life filled with losses to disease, Louis had proved that it was possible to conquer any disease caused by germs.

Afterword

In December 1892, representatives from many countries came to France to celebrate Louis's seventieth birthday, showering him with gifts and medals. They even presented a transparent crystal filled with glass "microbes" to the scientist who had made germs a household word.

Having suffered another stroke, Louis asked his son to read his speech. Louis remembered what his father had told him when he was a boy. He urged, "Ask: 'What have I done for my country?' until the time comes when you may have the immense happiness of thinking that you have contributed in some way to the progress and good of humanity."

Louis's research had run up against walls again and again. But he always kept trying until he transformed the walls into bridges leading to the answers he was determined to find. He had served his country, and all humanity, by discovering how to conquer diseases. And he intended to continue his work.

In April 1895, Louis became excited about plague germs that another scientist had just identified. Despite his failing health, he insisted on being carried to his laboratory. He studied the germs with delight, planning new research. But it would be the last time he ever looked into a microscope. Another stroke felled him in June. Louis weakened through the summer and died in September. He was buried in the cellar of the Pasteur Institute, the research laboratory he had founded. When Marie died in 1910, she was buried beside him.

Many medical developments of the 1900s were based on the ideas and research that Louis pioneered. His determination to find the right force to overpower harmful microbes stayed focused on one goal. "The purpose of scientific research," he always insisted, "is the improvement of human health." His success in conquering germs should be toasted whenever a person raises a glass of healthy milk that has been pasteurized.

Glossary

germ: a living thing that causes disease and is so small that it can be seen only with a microscope

microbe: a living thing that is so small that it can be seen only with a microscope

naturalist: in the 1800s, a scientist who believed that living things could develop from nonliving things

organism: a living thing

parasite: a living thing that lives on or inside another living thing and gets food from it

pasteurization: killing germs in a liquid by heating it to a certain temperature for a certain amount of time

spontaneous generation: an idea that states that living things could develop from nonliving things. This idea was proven to be false during the mid–1800s.

sterilize: to make an object or liquid free of living things by boiling or cleaning it

vaccine: a weakened germ that is injected into a person or animal to prevent the disease that the germ would cause at full strength

Selected Bibliography

Cuny, Hilaire. *Louis Pasteur: The Man and His Theories.* Translated by Patrick Evans. London: Souvenir Press, 1965.

Debré, Patrice. *Louis Pasteur.* Translated by Elborg Forster. Baltimore, MD: Johns Hopkins University Press, 1994.

de Kruif, Paul. *Microbe Hunters.* New York: Harcourt Brace & Company, 1926.

Dubois, René. *Louis Pasteur: Free Lance of Science.* New York: Little, Brown, 1950.

Farley, John. *The Spontaneous Generation Controversy from Descartes to Oparin.* Baltimore, MD: Johns Hopkins University Press, 1977.

Geison, Gerald L. *The Private Science of Louis Pasteur.* Princeton, NJ: Princeton University Press, 1995.

Latour, Bruno. *The Pasteurization of France.* Cambridge, MA: Harvard University Press, 1988.

Vallery-Radot, René. *The Life of Pasteur.* Translated by R. L. Devonshire. New York: Dover Publications, 1901.

The quotations in this book are translated by the author from the letters of Louis and Marie Pasteur and the works of Maurice Vallery-Radot and René Vallery-Radot.

Index

About the Author

Elaine Marie Alphin loves to discover the fascinating stories behind the people and things that changed history. While writing *Germ Hunter*, she read many of Louis and Marie Pasteur's letters in the original French, translating them herself for this book. Ms. Alphin has written more than twenty books for young readers, including *Davy Crockett, Telephones, Toasters*, and *Vacuum Cleaners*. Her award-winning fiction includes *Ghost Soldier*, which was nominated for the 2002 Edgar Allan Poe Award, Best Juvenile Mystery category, and won the 2002 Society of Midland Authors Award for Children's Fiction. Readers can learn more about Ms. Alphin's books at <http://www.elainemariealphin.com>.

About the Illustrator

Elaine Verstraete has illustrated several biographies for young readers, including *Mother Teresa, Alexander Graham Bell*, and *Helen Keller*. Along with illustrating books, she teaches art classes and sells fine-art paintings. Ms. Verstraete lives in Bristol, New York.